THE BIG LISZT OF MUSIC JOKES

F. Adams

The Big Liszt of Music Jokes

By F. Adams

Contents

Introduction

Most professions have their own in-jokes but musicians, given to arrogance, pretension, bad housing, lack of sleep and far too much travelling, seem to have an *especially* large back-catalogue.

Most music humour is self-deprecating, well perhaps not so much *self* deprecating as abusing other musicians who have committed the unforgivable folly of choosing a different instrument or genre.

This book is a collection of well over 600 one liners, humorous lists and definitions spanning classical, rock, folk, jazz, country **and** western, mocking over 50 instruments and their players along the way. Not content with mocking musicians this book mocks drummers too.

Mocking Musicians and Music

Don't let your children watch symphonies on TV.

There's far too much sax and violins.

Middle C, E flat and G walk into a bar.

"Sorry." said the barman. "we don't serve minors."

Why was the music theorist drunk?

He added a fifth to his tonic.

What's the difference between a musician and a large pizza?

A pizza can feed a family of four.

Two back row orchestral players go fishing and one falls out of the boat.

"Help!" he screams "I don't know how to swim!"

His partner replies: "Just fake it!"

A young child says to his mother, "When I grow up I'd like to be a musician."

She replies, "Well honey, you know you can't do both."

Telling jokes about musicians is risky, some of them take notes.

How do you make musicians complain?

Pay them.

What's the difference between a puppy and a singer-songwriter?

Eventually the puppy stops whining.

What's the first thing a musician says at work?

"Would you like fries with that?"

The Theory of Relativity for Musicians:

E = Fb.

Why did Bono fall off the stage?

He was too close to The Edge.

How come U2 still haven't found what they're looking for?

Because the streets have no names.

How do you get a million dollar career from singing jazz?

Start with two million.

Why was the jazz band's insurance so high?

Too many accidentals.

There were two people walking down the street.

One of them was a musician, the other didn't have any money either.

What do you call a musician with a university degree?

Night manager at McDonalds.

Two men were at a bar and one said, "Hey, I had my IQ checked and it was 175."

The other responded "That's a coincidence, so is mine, what do you do for a living?"

"I'm a physicist." was the reply.

Again came "that's a coincidence so am I."

This was overheard at a nearby table and these two compared IQ's at 160 and were surprised to learn that they were both brain surgeons.

At another nearby table one man despondently said to the other "Did you hear that? I had my IQ checked and it was only 52."

The other said, rather enthusiastically, "That's a coincidence. So is mine. What instrument do you play????"

Why do musicians have to be awake by six o'clock?

Because most shops close by six thirty.

What's the difference between bebop and a dixieland musicians?

The bebop musician flats his fifth, the dixieland musician drinks his.

How does a young man become a member of a high school chorus?

On the first day of school he turns into the wrong classroom.

What is the difference between war and a high school chorus?

The high school chorus causes more suffering.

Why do high school choruses travel so often?

It keeps assassins guessing.

What's the definition of an optimist?

A choral director with a mortgage.

What is the difference between a high school choral director and a chimpanzee?

It's scientifically proven that chimpanzees are able to communicate with humans.

Retweet this if your favourite key is G major - #F

Why did Santa Claus go to music college?

To improve his wrapping skills.

What did Jay-Z call his wife before they got married?

Feyonce.

What do you call a gingerbread man with one leg bitten off?

Limp Bizkit.

Why are jazz musicians so upbeat?

Two Beach Boys walk into a bar:

"Round?"

"Round."

"Get a round?"

"I'll get a round."

How many record producers does it take to change a light bulb?

Two. One to tell the engineer to do it, the other to say "I don't know, what do you think?"

What happens when you play the blues backwards?

Your wife comes back to you, your dog returns to life and you get out of prison.

What happens when you play country western music backwards?

You get your pickup truck back, your dog returns to life, and you get back your job at the car wash.

What does it say on a blues singer's tombstone?

"I didn't wake up this morning..."

Why do blues musicians tour the most in the summer?

So they can visit all their kids.

How many sound men does it take to change a light bulb?

1. "One, two, three, one, two, three…"
2. "Hey man, I just do sound."
3. One. Upon finding no replacement, he takes the original apart, repairs it with a chewing gum wrapper and duct tape, changes the screw mount to bayonet mount, finds an appropriate patch cable, and re-installs the bulb fifty feet from where it should have been, to the satisfaction of the rest of the band.

Puns related to the use of Italian words in music theory really aren't my forte.

What do you get when you put a diminished chord together with an augmented chord?

A demented chord.

My girlfriend said she was leaving me because of my obsession with the Monkees.

I thought she was joking, but then I saw her face.

Saint Peter is checking ID's at the Pearly Gates, and first comes a Texan. "Tell me, what have you done in life?" says St. Peter.

The Texan says, "Well, I struck oil, so I became rich, but I didn't rest on my laurels. I divided all my money among my entire family in my will, so our descendants are all set for about three generations."

St. Peter says, "That's quite something. Come on in. Next!"

The second guy in line has been listening, so he says, "I struck it big in the stock market, but I didn't selfishly just provide for my own like that Texan guy. I donated five million to Save the Children."

"Wonderful!" says Saint Peter. "Come in. Who's next?"

The third guy has been listening, and says timidly with a downcast look, "Well, I only made five thousand dollars in my entire lifetime."

"Goodness!" says St. Peter. "What instrument did you play?"

A Martian walks into a music store and says: "take me to your lieder."

A musician was asked: "What is the capital of Hawaii?" He replies: "H".

Composers

What is Beethoven's favourite fruit?

Ba-na-na-naaaaa.

The key to Beethoven's success was his understanding that if it ain't baroque, don't fix it.

Why couldn't the string quartet find their composer?

He was Haydn.

Arnold Schwarzenegger was invited to a composer's fancy dress party.

When asked who he was going as, he replied: "I'll be Bach."

There are so many jokes about composers.

I could write you a Liszt.

Beethoven had an ear for music.

Knock knock.
Who's there?
Philip Glass.
Knock knock.
Who's there?
Philip Glass.
Knock knock.
Who's there?
Philip Glass.
Knock knock.
Who's there?
Philip Glass.
Knock knock.
Who's there?
Philip Glass.
Knock knock.
Who's there?
Philip Glass.

Some people see the glass is half empty, while others see the glass as half full. Most people just hate Philip Glass.

What do most musicians do when they hear Philip Glass?

The ask: "Red or white?"

Did you hear about that composer who committed suicide?

He didn't even leave a note.

Wagner's music has beautiful moments, but some *really* bad quarters of an hour.

Did you hear about the composer who could only compose in 3/4 time?

He had Waltz-timers disease.

We've all heard of the so-called "Mozart Effect" based on the 1993 study that showed that students performed better on a spatial reasoning test after listening to a recording of Mozart.

What effects though, might other composers have on children?

The Mozart Effect:

Makes a child cleverer and more mathematical along with a higher IQ

The Haydn Effect:

Child is witty and quick on his feet, often bringing a grin to the faces of those around him. Despite this he exhibits remarkable humility.

The Bach Effect:

Child memorises Scripture and says his prayers every day; may overwhelm listeners with his speech.

The Handel Effect:

Like the Bach Effect; the child may also exhibit dramatic behaviour.

The Beethoven Effect:

Child develops a superiority complex and is prone to violent tantrums; is a perfectionist.

The Liszt Effect:

Child speaks rapidly and extravagantly, but never really says anything important.

The Bruckner Effect:

Child speaks very slowly and repeats himself frequently. Gains a reputation for profundity.

The Grieg Effect:

This child is quirky yet cheery. May be prone toward Norwegian folklore.

The Wagner Effect:

Child becomes a megalomaniac. Speaks for six hours at a stretch.

The Schoenberg Effect:

Child never repeats a word until he has used all the other words in his vocabulary. Sometimes talk backwards or upside-down. Eventually people stop listening to him. Child blames them for their inability to understand him.

The Ives Effect:

Child develops a remarkable ability to carry on several separate conversations at once.

The Stravinsky Effect:

Child is prone to savage, guttural and profane outbursts that lead to fighting and pandemonium in preschool.

The Shostakovich Effect:

Child only expresses themselves in parent-approved ways.

The Cage Effect:

Childs says exactly nothing for 4 minutes and 33 seconds. Preferred by 9 out of 10 classroom teachers.

The Glass Effect:

Child repeats one word over, and over, and over, and over....

Conductors

How many conductors does it take to screw in a light bulb?

No one knows, no one ever looks at him.

What do you call a hundred conductors at the bottom of the Ocean?

A good start.

What is the difference between a conductor and God?

God doesn't think he's a conductor.

What was the former conductor of the Berlin Philharmonic always first off the plane?

Because he only had Karajan luggage.

What's the difference between alto clef and Greek?

Some conductors actually read Greek.

What do you have when a group of conductors are up to their necks in wet concrete?

Not enough concrete.

What do all great conductors have in common?

They're all dead.

If you see a conductor and a violist in the middle of the road, who would you run over first?

The conductor, business before pleasure.

What's the perfect weight of a conductor?

Three and one-half pounds, including the urn.

If Hitler, Stalin and a conductor all walked into the room in which you were standing, and you had a gun but only two bullets, who would you shoot first?

The conductor... twice.

Why are conductor's hearts so coveted for transplants?

They've had so little use.

I know a guy who was so stupid his teacher gave him two sticks and he became a drummer, but then lost one and had to become a conductor.

What's black and brown and looks good on a conductor?

A Rottweiler.

Instruction manual for conductor:

Wave stick until the music stops, then turn around and bow.

A musician calls the symphony office to talk to the conductor.

"I'm sorry, he's dead," comes the reply.

The musician calls back 25 times, always getting the same reply from the receptionist.

At last she asks him why he keeps calling. He replies "I just like to hear you say it."

A blind rabbit and a blind snake bump into each other in the forest.

The rabbit said, "Watch where you are going. Can't you see that I am blind?"

The snake replied. "No. I can't see that you're blind because I'm blind myself."

Then the rabbit had a brilliant idea. "Why don't we feel each other and guess what the other is?"

The snake accepted this proposal and went first.

The snake said, "Let's see – you're furry with long ears and a cotton tail - you must be a rabbit."

"Very good," said the rabbit. "Now it's my turn. You are cold, slimy, spineless and have no ears. You must be a conductor."

Did you hear that some Yttrium barium copper oxide got a job leading the London Symphony Orchestra?

It was a superconductor.

Singers

General

What's the first sign of madness?

Suggs walking up your driveway.

I called my laptop "Hello", because it's a Dell.

Why couldn't Anthony Kiedis get his DVD player to work.

Scart issue.

How can you tell if a singer is at your door?

They can't find the key and they never know when to come in.

It must be terrible for an opera singer to realise that he can never sing again.

Yes, but it's much more terrible if he doesn't realise it.

A pianist and singer are rehearsing "Autumn Leaves" for a concert and the pianist says:

"OK. We will start in G minor and then on the third bar, modulate to B major and go into 5/4.

When you get to the bridge, modulate back down to F# minor and alternate a 4/4 bar with a 7/4 bar.

On the last A section go into double time and slowly modulate back to G minor."

The singer says: "Wow, I don't think I can remember all of that."

The pianist says: "Well, that's what you did last time."

Folk Singers

How many Folk Singers does it take to change a light bulb?

One to change it and 5 to sing about how good the old one was.

I'm glad Bob Dylan won the Nobel Prize in Literature.

I'm not sure how I'd feel about Dr. Dre winning the Nobel Prize in Medicine.

Sopranos

How does a soprano sing a scale?

Do re mi me me me me ME!

How many sopranos does it take to change a light bulb?

One. She just holds on and the world revolves around her.

What's the difference between a soprano and a pit bull?

Lipstick.

What's the difference between a Wagnerian soprano and a Wagnerian Tenor?

About 10 pounds.

What's the difference between a soprano and a terrorist?

You can negotiate with a terrorist.

What is the difference between a soprano and a cobra?

One is deadly poisonous, and the other is a reptile.

If you threw a violist and a soprano off a cliff, which one would hit the ground first?

1. The violist. The soprano would have to stop halfway down to ask directions.
2. Who cares?

How is a soprano different from a sewer rat?

Some people actually like sewer rats.

How do you tell if a Wagnerian soprano is dead?

The horses seem very relieved.

What's the definition of an alto?

A soprano who can sight read.

How do you put a sparkle in a soprano's eye?

Shine a torch in her ear.

How many sopranos does it take to change a light bulb?

Two. One to change it and one to watch and say, "Don't you think that's a bit high for you, dear?"

How many sopranos does it take to change a light bulb?

None; she thinks it's the accompanist's job.

Did you hear about the soprano who had quite a range at the lower end of the scale.

She was known as the deep C diva.

Sopranos defy the laws of astrophysics?

The centre of the universe shifts with every step they take.

Tenors

Did you hear about the Tenor who was so arrogant that the other Tenors noticed?

What's the definition of a male quartet?

Three men and a tenor.

How do you tell if a tenor is dead?

The wine bottle is still full and the comics haven't been touched.

How many tenors does it take to change a light bulb?

Four. One to change the bulb and three to bitch that they could have done it if they had the high notes.

Where is a tenor's resonance?

Where his brain should be.

If you took all the tenors in the world and laid them end to end, it would be a good idea.

What is the definition of an octave?

An octave can be described as having eight diatonic steps, twelve chromatic steps, or twenty-seven when sung by a tenor.

A hard up flautist was fed up with the poor employment prospects and decided to give up and start an opera company.

He was so poor that he had to resort to bartering for singers: "I can give you two fifes for a tenor."

How can you tell when a tenor is really stupid?

When the other tenors notice.

Why do tenors never say anything bad about musicians?

Because they're too busy talking about themselves.

Choristers Guide To Keeping Conductors In Line

The basic training of every singer should, of course, include myriad types of practical and theoretical emphases. One important area which is often neglected, however, is the art of one-upmanship.

The following rules are intended as guides to the development of habits which will promote the proper type of relationship between singer and conductor.

1. Never be satisfied with the starting pitch. If the conductor uses a pitch-pipe, make known your preference for pitches from the piano and vice-versa.
2. Complain about the temperature of the rehearsal room, the lighting, crowded space, and of a draft. It's best to do this when the conductor is under pressure.
3. Bury your head in the music just before cues.
4. Ask for a re-audition or seating change. Ask often. Give the impression you're about to quit. Let the conductor know you're there as a personal favour.
5. Loudly clear your throat during pauses (tenors are trained to do this from birth). Quiet instrumental interludes are a good chance to blow your nose.
6. Long after a passage has gone by, ask the conductor if your C# was in tune. This is especially effective if you had no C# or were not singing at the time.
7. At dramatic moments in the music (which the conductor is emoting), be busy marking your music so that the climaxes will sound empty and disappointing.
8. Wait until well into a rehearsal before letting the conductor know that you don't have the music.
9. Look at your watch frequently. Shake it in disbelief occasionally.

10. When possible, sing your part either an octave above or below what is written. This is excellent ear-training for the conductor. If he hears the pitch, deny it vehemently and claim that it must have been the combination tone.
11. Tell the conductor, "I can't find the beat." Conductors are always sensitive about their "stick technique" so challenge it frequently.
12. If you are singing in a language with which the conductor is the least bit unfamiliar, ask her as many questions as possible about the meaning of individual words. If this fails, ask her about the pronunciation of the most difficult words. Occasionally, say the word twice and ask her preference, making to say it exactly the same both times. If she remarks on their similarity, give her a look of utter disdain and mumble under your breath about the "subtleties of inflection".
13. Ask the conductor if he has listened to the von Karajan recording of the piece. Imply that he could learn a thing or two from it. Also good: ask, "Is this the first time you've conducted this piece?"
14. If your articulation differs from that of others singing the same phrase, stick to your guns. Do not ask the conductor which is correct until backstage just before the concert.
15. Find an excuse to leave the rehearsal about 15 minutes early so that others will become restless and start to fidget.

Make every effort to take the attention away from the podium and put it on you, where it belongs!

Instruments of Torture an A to Z

Accordion

What's the definition of perfect pitch?

When you toss a banjo in the bin and it hits an accordion.

What's a bassoon good for?

Kindling for an accordion fire.

What's a accordion good for?

Learning how to fold a map.

Whats the difference between terrorists and accordion players?

Terrorists have sympathisers.

What's the difference between an Uzi and an accordion?

The Uzi stops after 20 rounds.

What do you call ten accordions at the bottom of the ocean?

A good start.

Did you hear the joke about polka music?

I don't remember how it goes, but the punchline is "the accordion player got hit by a car".

What's the difference between an accordion and a concertina?

The accordion takes longer to burn.

Minimum safe distances between street musicians and the public:

- Violinist: 25 feet
- Bad Violinist: 50 feet
- Tone Deaf Guitar Player who knows 3 chords: 75 feet
- 15 year-old Electric Guitar Player with Nirvana fixation: 100 feet
- Accordionist: 60 miles

How do you protect a valuable instrument?

Hide it in an accordion case.

An accordion is a bagpipe with pleats.

How many accordions can you fit in a telephone box?

101 if you chop them finely enough.

What is the song most requested of accordionists?

Can you play Far, Far Away.

What's the difference between an accordion and a macaw?

One is loud, obnoxious and noisy; the other is a bird.

Did you hear about the unemployed accordion player?

He couldn't make ends meet.

Did you hear about the accordion player haunted by a malevolent spirit?

It turned out to be polkageist.

Aeolian Harp

Playing the aeolian harp is a breeze.

I learned to play the aeolian harp by air.

That aeolian harp player sucked.

How does Bob Dylan play the aeolian harp?

The answer, my friend, is blowing in the wind.

Appalachian Dulcimer

What's the difference between an Appalachian dulcimer and a hammered dulcimer?

A hammered dulcimer burns hotter; an Appalachian dulcimer burns longer.

When other musicians complain because the dulcimer is too loud… and there's only the one player.

You know you own too many dulcimers when:

- You start using them as bird houses.
- You put one in a pond just to see how well it floats.
- You can't afford to change the strings on all of them.
- You keep one on your desk to hold pens and pencils in the sound holes.
- You can't count them all without loosing track.

Why do people always pick on the banjo player?

Because there's no dulcimer player in the group.

Why do people always pick on the banjo player?

Because there's no dulcimer player in the group.

When a dulcimer player goes out busking, they throw money in the case when he is NOT playing.

Marriage is like playing the dulcimer. It looks easy until you try it.

What does a dulcimer and a baseball have in common?

People cheer when you hit them with a bat.

I went up to see my friend in the hospital the other day.

We chatted a bit, then I played a couple songs on my dulcimer.

When it was time to go, I said "Well, I hope you get better!"

My friend said - "Yeah - I hope you do too"!

An Appalachian dulcimer goes into a bar and says "Barman, give me ten beers."

The barman says "Hey buddy, why are you drinking so much?"

The dulcimer replies "Because I want to be a hammered dulcimer."

Bagpipes

How do you get two bagpipers to play a perfect unison? Shoot one.

Heck, shoot both!

How is playing a bagpipe like throwing a javelin blindfolded?

You don't have to be very good to get people's attention.

If you drop an accordion, a set of bagpipes and a viola off a 20-story building, which one lands first?

Who cares?

Why do bagpipe players walk while they play?

To get away from the noise.

Why do bagpipers always walk when they play?

Moving targets are harder to hit.

How can you tell if a bagpipe is out of tune?

Someone is blowing into it.

Angus was asked why there were drones on the bagpipe when they make such a distressing sound.

He answered, "Without the drones, I might as well be playing the piano."

Did you hear the joke invented by a drunk Irishman?

It's called the bagpipes and the Scots still don't get it.

Why did the bagpipe player cross the road?...... I thought while accelerating.

What do you call a successful bagpiper?

A guy whose wife has 2 jobs.

What's the definition of a quarter tone?

A bagpiper tuning his drones.

How can you tell a bagpiper with perfect pitch?

He can throw a set into the middle of a pond and not hit any of the ducks.

A group of terrorists hijacked a plane full of bagpipers.

They called ground control with a list of demands. Then they told the negotiator if their demands aren't met they will release one bagpiper an hour.

A man in a kilt walks into a pub with a plastic bag under his arms and the bartender asks, "What's that?"

"Six pounds of Semtex", he answers.

"That's a relief. I thought it was bagpipes."

A Canadian officer, pinned down with his unit in Italy in 1944, urgently signalled his CO - "Need reinforcements to rescue us. Please send six tanks or one piper."

What do you throw a drowning bagpiper?

His bagpipes....

When someone tells a guitarist joke, people laugh.

When someone tells a bagpipe joke, people nod in solemn agreement.

How can you tell one pipe tune from another?

By the titles.

How do you put a twinkle in a piper's eye?

Shine a light in his ear.

The drone strike terrorist fear the most comes from the pipes of the Black Watch.

What's the difference between a dead snake in the road and a dead bagpiper in the road?

Skid marks in front of the snake.

Banjo

Why do some people have an instant aversion to banjo players?

It saves time in the long run.

How many banjo players does it take to screw in a light bulb?

Five. One to screw it in and four ask what tuning he's using.

Why was the banjo player staring intently at the carton of orange juice?

Because it said "Concentrate".

What's the difference between a banjo and a chain saw?

The chain saw has greater dynamic range.

What will you never say about a banjo player?

"That's the banjo player's Porsche."

How are a banjo player and a blind javelin thrower alike?

Both command immediate attention and alarm, and force everyone to move out of range.

What do Beethoven and Schubert have in common?

They both don't play the banjo.

How many banjo players does it take to screw in a light bulb?

Five. One to screw it in and four to argue about what year it was made.

There's nothing I like better than the sound of a banjo, unless of course it's the sound of a chicken caught in a vacuum cleaner.

What is the banjo picker's favourite wine?

"Play Duelling Banjos…"

What's the best or fastest way to tune a banjo?

With wire cutters.

Female five string banjoist shouting at her boyfriend in a crowded shopping mall: "Don't forget, sweetheart, I need a new G string."

How many banjo players does it take to screw in a light bulb?

Five. One to screw it in and four to complain that it's electric.

What's the difference between a fiddle and a violin?

Who cares! Neither of them is a banjo!

How do you keep a banjo player in suspense?…

Banjos are to music what Etch-a-Sketch is to art.

A man walked into a bar with his alligator and asked the bartender "Do you serve banjo players here?"

"Sure do," replied the bartender.

"Good," said the man.

"Give me a beer, and I'll have a banjo picker for my 'gator."

Why was the banjo player standing on the roof?

Because they told him the drinks were on the house.

Santa Claus, the tooth fairy, a good banjo player, and an old drunk are walking down the street together when they simultaneously spot a hundred dollar bill.

Who gets it?

The old drunk, of course, the other three are mythological creatures.

A banjo player walked into a bar…

Another banjo player walked into the bar…

You'd think the second banjo player would have seen what happened to the first banjo player and ducked!

What is the best sort of relationship to have with a banjo player?

No strings attached.

Banjo Tuning is an oxymoron.

A man went to a brain store to get some brain for dinner. He sees a sign remarking on the quality of brain offered at this particular brain store, so he asks the butcher: "How much for fiddle player brain?"

"2 dollars an ounce."

"How much for mandolin player brain?"

"3 dollars an ounce."

"How much for guitar player brain?"

"4 dollars an ounce."

"How much for banjo player brain?"

"100 dollars an ounce."

"Why is banjo player brain so much more?"

"Do you know how many banjo players you need to kill to get one ounce of brain?"

What has 16 legs and 3 teeth?

The front row of a banjo workshop.

Banjo players won't play just any type of music, they can be quite picky.

A bluegrass band is on their way back from a gig South of the border when they get arrested for playing a banjo after dark.

The judge quickly sentences them to death.

At dawn the next morning the band finds themselves looking at the business end of a firing squad.

"Ready, Aim,..."

"Earthquake!" yells the guitar player, which distracts the guards long enough so he can jump over the wall to freedom.

"Ready, Aim,..."

"Flood!" yells the mandolin player who jumps over the wall to freedom.

Now the banjo player is starting to catch on.

"Ready, Aim,..."

"Fire!" yells the banjo player as loud as he can...

Why do banjo players like family reunions?

It's a great place to pick up girls.

A banjo player was so poor that he couldn't afford lessons, so his friends chipped in and got him banjo lessons for his birthday.

They sent the greatest banjo teacher that every lived to his house.

The teacher knocked on the door and said "I'm here to give you Super Playing Abilities!"

The banjo player replied "I'll take the soup, I haven't had dinner yet…"

A guy goes through customs with a banjo case.

The inspector nervously asks the man to set the case on the table.

Sweating, the inspector uses a long stick to slowly open the case.

He sighs in relief when the contents reveal a machine gun and miscellaneous explosives.

"Phew! For a minute there, I thought you had a banjo…"

Banjo player: "When I die, I want to leave the world a better place."

Guitar player: "Don't worry, you will."

Banjo Tab:

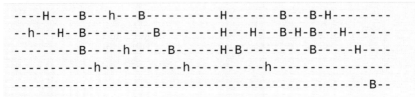

```
----H----B---h---B----------H-------B---B-H--------
--h---H--B---------B-------H---H---B-H-B---H-----
--------B----h-----B------H-B--------B-----H----
----------h----------h---------h---------------
--------------------------------------------B--
```

h = hit it! H = hit it harder! B = beat it!

Two banjo players walk into a bar.

One says "Did you hear about the Brazilian soldiers killed today?"

His friend replies "Jeez... that's TERRIBLE! Um... how many's in a brazillion?"

What's the most beautiful sound a banjo can make?

"Splash".

What's worse than a banjo?

Banjos.

Bass

Did you hear about the bassist who was so out of tune his section noticed?

Bass... the lowest form of music.

How do you get two bass players to play in unison?

Hand them charts a half-step apart.

What do you do if you run over a bass player?

Back up.

What do you throw a drowning bass player?

His amp.

What do you call a guitar that's made of sodium hydroxide?

Base guitar.

What do you call a bass player who only knows two chords?

A professional.

How do you make a double bass sound in tune?

Chop it up and make it into a xylophone.

183 bass players walked into a bar and ordered drinks.

The bartender told them, "I don't serve liquor to bass players."

They answered, "It's okay. We'll just stick to tonic."

A father was buying bass lessons for his son.

On the 1st week the father asked what he had learned. The son said "On my 1st lesson we learned about the E string."

The 2nd week came and again the father asked what had he learned. The son replied "On my 2nd lesson I learned about the A string."

3rd week came by and the father said to his son "You know these are expensive lessons what have you learned this week?"

The son said "I quit the lessons, I've already got a gig."

How many bass players does it take to change a light bulb?

1…5…1… (1…4…5…5…1)

A double bass player arrived a few minutes late for the first rehearsal of the local choral society's annual performance of Handel's Messiah.

He picked up his instrument and bow, and turned his attention to the conductor.

The conductor asked, "Would you like a moment to tune?"

The bass player replied with some surprise, "Why? Isn't it the same as last year?"

At a rehearsal, the conductor stops and shouts to the bass section: "You are out of tune. Check it, please!"

The first bassist pulls all his strings, says, "Our tuning is correct: all the strings are equally tight."

The first violist turns around and shouts, "You idiot! It's not the tension. The pegs have to be parallel!"

Bassoon

What's the difference between a bassoon and a trampoline?

You take your shoes off to jump on a trampoline.

What's the difference between an oboe and a bassoon?

You can hit a cricket ball further with a bassoon.

How do you insult a saxophone player?

Call him a bassoonist.

What's the advantage a bassoon has over an oboe?

It burns longer.

Why did the chicken cross the road?

To get away from the bassoon recital.

Why don't bassoonists ever catch a cold?

Even viruses have pride.

What's the difference between a bassoon and a lawnmower?

You don't pour petrol ON the lawnmower.

How do you join a community orchestra as a bassoon player?

Own a bassoon.

Why shouldn't you take the bassoon section on a pub crawl?

They are always a bar behind.

How do you get 100 bassoonists into a phone box?

Throw in a food stamp.

How do you get them out?

Throw in a bar of soap.

Bodhrán

What do you call a groupie who hangs around and annoys musicians?

A bodhrán player.

There was the fiddle player who, while visiting the local pub, was asked for a Euro to help pay for the funeral of a local bodhrán player.

"Here's two Euro;" he says "bury another."

How do you know when there is a bodhrán player at your front door?

The knocking gets faster and faster and faster.

What's the best thing to play a bodhrán with?

A razor blade.

What's the definition of an optimist?

A bodhrán player with an answering machine.

What do you call a bodhrán player with a broken wrist?

A huge improvement.

Bodhrán care is simple… Rub gently with lighter fluid and ignite.

Best things to do with a bodhrán:

- Set fire to the hoop and make the player jump through it.
- Roll it over a cliff into the ocean.
- Nail soup can lids around the rim and use it as a tambourine.

Customer: I'd like to buy a guitar, please.

Shop Assistant: You're a bodhrán player, aren't you?

Customer: How did you know that?

Shop Assistant: This is a fish and chip shop.

How many bodhrán players does it take to change a light bulb?

20 One to hold the bulb and the remaining 19 to drink until the room spins.

What's the difference between a flat tyre and a bodhrán?

One makes an irregular thumping sound, is difficult to work with and interferes with smooth progress, and the other, uhhh, err, uhhhh, hmmm…

How can you tell if a bodhrán player has been doing a crossword?

All the squares have been coloured in.

How are bodhráns more useful than other instruments?

You can boil them up for swill.

What's the only thing more satisfying than seeing seven bodhráns in a dustbin?

Seeing one bodhrán in seven dustbins.

What's the difference between endangered tropical rainforest mahogany and a bodhrán?

I don't have mahogany in my fireplace.

Bongo

What do you call two nuns playing a bongo?

A conundrum.

Bongos remind me of children.

They're slightly annoying, rich people bring them back from Africa, and if you beat them in public then people get angry.

Why was the bongo arrested holding a pair of binoculars?

He was a peeping tom-tom.

What's the most effective male contraceptive?

Telling a girl you play the bongos.

A bongo player is like an appendix.

They can both be a big pain sometimes, you don't miss them when they're gone, and no one's quite figured out what good they are.

Cello

How do you get a 'cellist to play fortissimo?

Write "pp, espressivo".

How do you make a cello sound beautiful?

Sell it and buy a violin.

Why is a cello solo like a bomb?

By the time you hear it, it's too late to do anything about it.

What's the difference between a cello and a coffin?

The coffin has the dead person on the inside.

What's the difference between a chainsaw and a cello?

If you absolutely had to, you could use a chainsaw in a string quartet.

Why can't you hear a cello on a digital recording?

Recording technology has reached such an advanced level of development that all extraneous noise is eliminated.

Why is playing the cello like peeing in your pants?

They both give you a nice warm feeling without making any sound.

Why do cellists leave their instrument cases on the dashboards of their cars?

Because if someone mistakes them for mafia, they might get some respect.

How do you get a violin to sound like a cello?

Play in the low register with a lot of wrong notes.

Why shouldn't you drive off a cliff in a minivan with three cellos in it?

You could fit in at least one more.

Did you hear about the cellist who bragged that he could play 32nd notes?

The rest of the orchestra didn't believe him, so he proved it by playing one.

How do you transcribe a viola piece for cello?

Divide the metronome marking by 2.

A violinist noticed at the end of each rehearsal break, one of the cellists would look at the inside flap of his jacket before he sat down to resume rehearsal.

This continued for several decades, and the violinist became quite curious about it.

One day, during hot weather, the cellist took off his jacket and went off on break.

The violinist waited until everyone was off the platform, looked around, and sneaked over to the jacket.

He pulled back the flap and saw a little note pinned on the inside.

It read: "Cello left hand, bow right."

What is the difference between a cello and an anchor?

You tie a rope to an anchor before you throw it overboard.

How do you get a cello to play in tune?

Tell him the key signature has 8 sharps.

What's this: X X X ?

Three cellists co-signing a loan.

What do you call a musician at a cello competition?

A visitor.

I recently had surgery on my hand, and asked the doctor if, after surgery, I would be able to play the cello. He said, "I'm doing surgery on your hand, not giving you a lobotomy."

How many strings does a cello have?

Four too many.

Chang

How long does it take to tune a chang?

Nobody knows.

Why is it so difficult to tune a chang?

So that violist can feel superior about something.

How many chang players does it take to change a light bulb?

All of them. One to twist the bulb for several hours, and the other one to decide that it's as good as it's going to get, and that they might as well flip the switch.

Clarinet

What do clarinetists use for contraception?

Their personalities.

What's the definition of "nerd?"

Someone who owns his own alto clarinet.

Why do clarinetists leave their cases on the dashboard?

So they can park in the handicapped zones.

How do you get a clarinetist out of a tree?

Cut the noose.

How many clarinetists does it take change a light bulb?

Only one, but they'll go through an entire box before they find the right one.

What do you call a bass clarinetist with half a brain?

Gifted.

Why did the clarinet player marry the accordion player?

Upward mobility.

If a clarinetist messes up the conductor will reed him the riot act.

What's the difference between a sports writer and a clarinetist?

The sports writer knows the score.

A clarinetist was involved in a car crash.

In her insurance claim form she blamed it on the reed.

Most clarinetists can't even reed music.

Cornet

Three big headed cornetists are on tour, travelling in an aeroplane, one says "I'm throwing a fifty pound note out to make someone happy".

The next says "I'm going to throw out 2 twenties and make 2 people happy".

The third said "Well I'm going to throw out 5 tens, It'll make 5 people happy".

Their conductor tells them " why don't you just all jump, and make the whole band happy?"

How do you get a cornet player to play treble forte?

Write *mp* on the part.

I used to play in a brass band specialising in REM covers.

That's me on the cornet.

Drums

How many drummers does it take to change a light bulb?

"oops, I broke it!"

What do you call a drummer in a three-piece suit?

"The Defendant".

What did the drummer get on his I.Q. Test?

Saliva.

What do you do if you see a bleeding drummer running around in your back yard?

Stop laughing and shoot again.

What does a drummer and a philosopher have in common?

They both perceive time as an abstract concept.

How do you know when a drummer is at your door?

He speeds up when he's knocking.

What's the difference between a drummer and a drum machine?

With a drum machine you only have to punch the information in once.

Heard backstage: "Will the musicians and the drummer please come to the stage!"

How do you get a drummer to play an accelerando?

Ask him to play in 4/4 at a steady 120 bpm.

Why do bands have bass players?

To translate for the drummer.

Why is it good that drummers have a half-ounce more brains than horses?

So they don't disgrace themselves in parades.

What is the difference between a drummer and a vacuum cleaner?

You have to plug the vacuum cleaner in before it sucks.

What's the last thing a drummer says before he gets kicked out of a band?

"When do we get to play MY songs?"

How can a drummer and a conductor avoid rhythm conflicts?

Work separate concert halls.

How can you tell if the stage is level?

The drool comes out of both sides of the drummers mouth.

What do you call someone who hangs around with musicians?

A drummer.

How many drummers does it take to screw in a bulb?

None, they have machines for that now.

Two drummers walk past a bar… nah it'll never happen.

How many drummers does it take to change a light bulb?

1. "Why? Oh, wow! Is it like dark, man?"
2. Only one, but he'll break ten bulbs before figuring out that they can't just be pushed in.
3. Two: one to hold the bulb, and one to turn his throne (but only after they figure out that you have to turn the bulb).
4. Twenty. One to hold the bulb, and nineteen to drink until the room spins.
5. None. They have a machine to do that.

What do you do with a drummer who has no sense of rhythm?

Take away one of sticks and make him the conductor.

Why are orchestra intermissions limited to 20 minutes?

So you don't have to retrain the drummers.

Did you hear about the time the bass player locked his keys in the car?

It took two hours to get the drummer out.

Didgeridoo

What do you call a didgeridoo that doesn't work?

A didgeridon't

I met this bloke with a didgeridoo and he was playing Dancing Queen on it.

I thought, that's Abba-riginal.

I was given a book, "How to play the didgeridoo."

All the pages are empty except one that says, "Far away from me."

What's a didgeridoo?

Whatever it wants to.

Did you hear about the didgeridoo player who had a brain transplant?

The brain rejected him a week later.

Dobro

What's black and blue and laying in a ditch?

A Dobro player who's told too many banjo jokes.

Is a Dobro player just a banjo player with a steel plate in his head?

Did you hear about the Dobro player who's so ugly that he shaves with his back to the mirror.

A Dobro player was in the city shopping at a department store when the power went out.

He was trapped on an escalator for three hours.

A Dobro player bought himself an A.M. radio.

It took him two weeks to figure out he could play it in the afternoon.

Those Dobro jokes really resonated with the banjo player.

Why do many bluegrass bands have Dobro players?

They need somewhere level to put their drinks.

How does a Dobro teacher charge for lessons?

On a sliding scale.

If a clarinetist plays clarinet, a French hornist plays a French horn, and a tubist plays a tuba, who plays a Dobro?

An idiot.

If a Dobro player and a banjo player caught a taxi, which one would be the musician?

The driver.

What's the difference between a Dobro player and a Duracell battery?

The Duracell battery has a good life.

Euphonium

How do you call a baritone player? euphonium.

What do you call a professional euphonium player who does not play in a military band?

Unemployed.

How many euphonium players does it take to change a light bulb?

What the heck's a euphonium?

What is the difference between euphonium players and baritone players?

Baritone players don't always whine about how they don't play euphonium!

How do you keep a euphonium player in suspense?

What instrument does the stupidest member of the band play?

Drums, but if that's too hard, they can always try euphonium.

How many euphonium players does it take to change a light bulb?

Two. One to hold the bulb and one to do breathing exercises until the room spins.

How do you make counterfeit baritone horns?

You phony 'em.

How does a Euphonium player make money?

By cleaning toilets.

baritone n:

1. vocal: someone who didn't make it as either a tenor or a bass;

2. instrumental: someone who didn't make it as either a tuba or a trombone;

3. a tuba that shrunk in the wash;

4. a trombone with taste;

5. an easier spelling of the word "euphonium."

Fiddle

What's the difference between a fiddle and a violin?

No-one minds if you spill beer on a fiddle.

Why do fiddlers pick on banjo players?

Because they can't pick on their fiddles.

It's a violin if you're selling it.

It's a fiddle if you're buying it.

How do you tell the difference between a violin and a fiddle?

Turn it over. If beer pours out, it's a fiddle.

Young fiddler to critic, after playing the Contradiction Reel (badly) :

"Yeah, that one was called "The Contradiction Reel"! Great, eh? A hard one to play, actually. What do you think of my execution?"

Critic : "I do hope it will be soon."

What's the difference between a fiddle and a violin?

The amount of alcohol involved.

Flugelhorn

How many flugelhorn players does it take to change a light bulb?

Five. One to stand on a chair and hold the bulb and 4 to rotate the chair.

Having played at a regional, I was watching a band drawn after us, who weren't doing too well.

I remarked to our trumpet player, "If they beat us, I'll sell my flugelhorn."

"So will I", he replied.

"Oh, I didn't know you had a flugelhorn," I said.

"I haven't," he replied, "I'd sell your flugelhorn as well."

Flute

How many flautists does it take to change a light bulb?

Just one, but he'll spend $5,000 on a Sterling silver bulb.

Guitar

What do call a guitarist without a girlfriend?

Homeless.

What do you call a guitarist that only knows two chords?

A music critic.

How many guitarist does it take to screw in a light bulb?

13 - one to do it, and twelve to stand around and say, "Pah! I can do that!"

How do you get a guitarist to play softer?

Place a sheet of music in front of him.

How many lead guitarists does it take to change a light bulb?

None, they just steal somebody else's light.

What do you call two guitarists playing in unison?

Counterpoint.

How many guitar players does it to take to change a light bulb?

Five. One to change and 4 to say they could have done it better.

Three guitarists collaborated on a book of scales.

Each contributed the one he knew.

What's the difference between a rock guitarist and a jazz guitarist?

A rock guitarist plays 3 chords in front of 3000 people and a jazz guitarist plays 3000 chords in front of 3 people.

What do a vacuum cleaner and an electric guitar have in common.

Both suck when you plug them in.

Relative minor: A guitarist's girlfriend.

In the 22th century, how many guitar players will you need to replace a light source?

Five. One to actually do it, and four to reminisce about how much better the old tubes were.

What's the difference between a BFF and a guitarist in a music shop?

The BFF bucks up their friends.

How can you tell if a classical guitarist is a dreamer?

He has an agent.

How can you tell if a classical guitarist is insane?

He has an agent and a publicist.

What is God's favourite guitar chord?

G sus.

Guitarists tend to fret a lot.

Harmonica

What is the range of a harmonica?

As far as you can throw it.

What do you call a harmonica player who says he knows what notes he's playing?

A Liar.

Why do dogs howl when harmonica players play?

They're trying to tell them how the song goes.

What do the best harmonica players have in common?

They all suck.

What do you say at the end of a great harmonica solo?

Thank God.

How Many Harmonic Players Does it take to change a light bulb?

Don't worry about the changes man, Just blow!

How many harmonica players does it take to screw in a light bulb?

Five. One to screw it in and four to determine if it should be in straight or cross position.

What do you call a harmonica player in a brand new suit?

Dearly departed.

What's the difference between a frog and a harmonica player?

The frog can read music.

Why do harmonica players say they play a "harp"?

"Harmonica" is a four-syllable word.

Harp

Why are harps like elderly parents?

Both are unforgiving and hard to get into and out of cars.

How long does a harp stay in tune?

About 20 minutes, or until someone opens a door.

What's the definition of a quarter tone?

A harpist tuning unison strings.

A harpist and an accordion player are playing a New Year's Eve gig at a local club.

The place is packed and everybody is absolutely loving the music.

Shortly after midnight, the club owner comes up to the duo and says, "You guys sound great, everybody loves you. I'd like to know if the two of you are free to come back here next New Year's Eve to play?

The two musicians look at each other then to the club owner and the harpist says "Sure, we'd love to, Is it OK if we leave our stuff here?"

Harpists tend to be quite feisty;

you could say that they have a lot of pluck.

Harpists' motto: "It's better to be sharp than out of tune."

Welcome to heaven; here's your harp and tuning key.

Welcome to hell; here's your harp.

What's the difference between a harpist and garbage?

The garbage gets taken out once a week.

Harpists tend to be highly-strung.

What do you get if you cross a grizzly bear and a harp?

A bear-faced lyre!

Harpsichord

Domenico Scarlatti wrote 555 harpsichord sonatas for which instrument?

———————◆⟨⟩◆———————

Which President can play the harpsichord?

Baroque Obama.

———————◆⟨⟩◆———————

Who tunes their A to 415?

Don't worry, you don't have to ask. They'll tell you.

Horn

How do you get a three piece horn section to play in tune?

Shoot two of them.

What do you get when you cross a French Horn player and a goalpost?

A goalpost that can't march.

How do you get a trumpet to sound like a French Horn?

Put your hand in the bell and play a lot of wrong notes.

Why is the French Horn a divine instrument?

Because a man blows in it, but only God knows what comes out of it.

How can you make a French Horn sound like a trombone?

1. Take your hand out of the bell and lose all sense of taste.
2. Take your hand out of the bell and miss all of the notes!

How do you get your viola section to sound like the horn section?

Have them miss every other note.

What is the difference between a French Horn section and a '57 Chevy?

You can tune a '57 Chevy.

How many French Horn players does it take to change a light bulb?

Just one, but he'll spend two hours checking the bulb for alignment and leaks.

What's the name of a good English Horn player?

I'll tell you when I meet one.

What do you call a Spanish cat who plays the French horn?

Le gato!

Hurdy-Gurdy

How long does it take to get a hurdy-gurdy in tune?

Nobody knows…

Irish Uilleann

Why are Uilleann Pipes the only instrument that would pass a vehicle inspection?

They have an air bag and seat belt!

How can you tell if Uilleann Pipes are out of tune?

Someone is working the bellows.

How did the Uilleann Piper dump his girlfriend?

He gave her the elbow.

Jew's harp

On which day did God invent the Jew's harp?

And couldn't he have rested on that day too?

Somebody gave a Jew's harp player a pair of water skis.

He threw them away as he couldn't find a lake with a hill in it.

Kazoo

Did you hear about the kazoo who married a doorbell?

They had a humdinger.

What's the difference between a kazoo and a wife?

One's a constant annoying noise in your ear and the other's a plastic trumpet!

Kettle Drum

A new conductor was at his first rehearsal. It was not going well.

He was wary of the musicians as they were of him.

As he left the rehearsal room, the timpanist sounded a rude little "bong."

The angry conductor turned and said, "All right! Who did that?"

Why did the string bass player get angry at the timpanist?

Because the timpanist turned a peg and wouldn't tell him which one.

Beethoven was extremely innovative for his time.

He would do things like timpani solos, which are the precursor to modern drum solos.

Of course, at the time, people were probably thinking "Timpani solo? Is this guy deaf?

There once was a timpinist who dreamed that he was playing in "Messiah" and when he woke up he was playing in "Messiah".

Lute

Lutenists spend half their time tuning their instrument and the other half playing out of tune.

A lutenist went to the pub for a drink, but the bouncer stopped him and said, "Sorry mate, you're bard."

Sonata for Cymbals and Lute in B-flat major. (I think the melodic line should be assigned to the cymbals.)

A group of thieves broke into a music shop.

They made off with the lute.

I had to take my lute into the luthier's because it was baroque.

Mandolin

What do you get when you cross a mandolin and a banjo?

An instrument that even a bass player can tell is out of tune.

Then there was the mandolin player who got addicted to playing waltzes. It was so bad, he had to go into rehab.

It was a three-step program!

Why does a mandolin have eight strings?

To double the chances that one of them will be in tune.

Why are mandolins so small?

So you can play it with handcuffs on!

Know why there was no mandolin music on Star Trek?

There are no mandolins in the future.

How do you recruit professional mandolin players in any large city?

Stand on a street corner and yell "Taxi!"

I knew that my first marriage was in trouble when my wife accused my of loving my mandolin more that I loved her.

My response at the time was; "Which mandolin?"

The banjo: an instrument that is synonymous with inbreeding.

The mandolin player didn't think that was funny. He shared it with his wife and sister and she didn't think it was funny either.

Two banjo players walked into a bar. The mandolin player ducked.

Marimba

I didn't like the marimba player very much.

He had bad vibes.

Melodeon

How do you pitch a melodeon?

As far into the sea as possible!

What's the difference between a melodeon and a cattle grid?

You drive slowly over a cattle grid.

I parked a Trabant with a melodeon on the back seat.

A car thief took the Trabant and left the melodeon on the pavement.

A chap bought a melodeon from a well known auction site.

When it arrived he found it would only play 'Staying Alive', 'Night Fever' & 'Massachusetts'.

Turns out it was a B/G melodeon.

What's the difference between a radio and a melodeon?

if you push the buttons on a radio, you could probably get a tune out of it!

Northumbrian Smallpipes

What's a bodhrán player's nightmare?

Three Northumbrian Smallpipers and a sitar player playing Balkan music, and a tabla player who can keep time with all of them.

What's the difference between the Northumbrian Smallpipe and the Great Highland Bagpipe?

The Northumbrian Smallpipe is a musical instrument"

Northumbrian Smallpipes...

the missing link between music and noise.

How do you kill a Northumbrian Smallpiper?

Fix his hearing aids.

Why do Northumbrian Smallpipers have such large families?

Their wives will do ANYTHING to get them to stop playing.

An elderly Northumbrian Smallpiper is playing while his wife watches.

"How long has he been playing the pipes?" a bystander asks the wife.

"Oh, about 60 years, but he spent 40 of those tuning them".

How do you plant dope?

Bury a Northumbrian Smallpiper.

How do you get a dozen Northumbrian Smallpipers to play in tune?

Who the hell wants a dozen Northumbrian Smallpipers?

What's the difference between an in-tune Northumbrian Smallpiper and Bigfoot?

Bigfoot has been spotted.

What's the difference between a Northumbrian Smallpiper and a walrus?

One squeals a lot and the other is a walrus.

Nose Flute

So I went to a music shop and said to the owner "can I see your kettle drum?"

He said "no, but would you like to hear my toaster play the nose flute?"

Oboe

How do you get an oboist to play A flat?

Take the batteries out of his electronic tuner.

What's the difference between a SCUD missile and a bad oboist?

A bad oboist can kill you.

A recording session ground to a halt when an oboe player, who was constantly sucking on her reed to keep it moist during rests and between takes, inadvertently inhaled and swallowed it.

The conductor immediately called 999 and asked what he should do. The operator replied, "Use muted trumpet instead."

What is a burning oboe good for?

Setting a bassoon on fire.

What is the definition of a major second?

Two baroque oboes playing in unison.

Organ

What does a Hammond organist do in his life's most tender moments?

He puts his Leslie on "slow".

A local church built a new sanctuary. They moved their very fine old pipe organ to the new sanctuary. It was an intricate task that was completed successfully.

The local news heralded… "St. Paul Completes Organ Transplant."

Fugue: There is an old saying that fugues are the type of music in which the voices come in one by one while the audience goes out one by one, but there is no statistical evidence to support this; audiences have been known to leave in droves.

Why doesn't heaven have a pipe organ?

Because they needed the keys in hell to make accordions.

Canon: Not to be confused with the ones required in the 1812 Overture which are spelt differently and which lack contrapuntal interest.

Piano

What do you get when you drop a piano down a mine shaft?

A flat minor.

What do you get when you drop a piano on an army base?

A flat major.

Why is a person who plays the piano called a pianist but a person who drives a racing car not called a racist?

Why was the pianist arrested?

Because he got into treble.

Did you hear about the stupid pianist who kept banging his head against the keys?

He was playing by ear.

A pianist went into a bar but kept fidgeting so much that he could not enjoy his drink.

Finally the bartender asked him what was wrong. The piano player replied, "My keys, my keys! I can't seem to find my keys!"

Did you hear about the vampire who used to torture his victims by playing piano to them?

His Bach was much worse than his bite.

Why are pianos so hard to open?

The keys are on the inside.

Piano Tuner: I've come to tune the piano.

Music Teacher: But we didn't send for you.

Piano Tuner: No, but the people who live across the street did.

Piccolo

What musical instrument would a cucumber play?

A pickle-o.

How do you make a piccolo player into a drummer?

Put another useless stick in their hand.

Quena

What's the best way to hold a quena?

With your Andes.

I told my wife I could play the quena.

She said "I don't Bolivia."

Did you hear about the quena player who went to a mind reader?

There was no charge.

Recorder

Don't stop, I was really enjoying your recorder practice. Said no parent, EVER!

They taught recorder to the kids who couldn't reed.

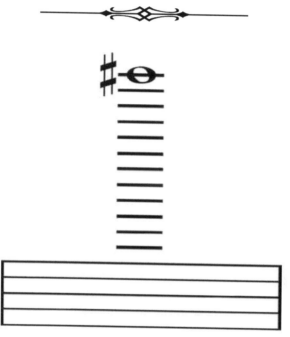

Saxophone

What's the difference between a chainsaw and a saxophone?

You can tune a chainsaw.

What's the difference between a baritone saxophone and a chain saw?

The exhaust.

It's small wonder we have so much trouble with air pollution in the world when so much of it has passed through saxophones.

What's the definition of a minor second interval?

Two Soprano Sax players reading the same part.

What's the definition of perfect pitch?

When the Saxophone lands in the MIDDLE of the skip.

How many alto sax players does it take to change a light bulb?

Five. One to change the bulb and four to contemplate how David Sanborn would have done it.

What's the difference between a saxophone and a lawn mower?

1. Lawn mowers sound better in small ensembles.
2. The neighbours are upset if you borrow a lawnmower and don't return it.
3. The grip.

Why did the lead alto player play so many wrong notes?

Because he kept ignoring the key signature – he thought it was a suggestion.

Why did Adolphe Sax invent the saxophone?

He hated mankind but couldn't build a atom bomb.

Sitar

I just got my best score on Sitar Hero 3!

I got five stars on "Curry On My Wayward Son"

What has 17 strings and attracts money and girls?

A sitar, OK I lied about the money and girls.

What was Ravi Shankar's favourite Sci-Fi programme?

Sitar Trek.

India has demanded that MTV apologise for airing "indecent" music videos.

MTV retaliated by demanding that India apologise for the sitar.

Theremin

you might be a thereminist if:

- your home and neighbourhood are devoid of all insects, vermin and domestic animals.
- your neighbourhood gets a lot of "sound only, nothing seen" UFO reports.
- most of your CD collection consists of sci-fi movie themes.
- you have ever used "Somebody got to close to me." as an excuse for hitting a wrong note.
- you ever waved you hands at another musical instrument and got frustrated with not being able to get it to play.
- you don't tip street musicians because they always put their tip jar way to close to themselves and you would have to reach through there control fields to leave a tip.
- your parents beg you not to practice.
- you dislike the radios they have for sale at a store because they only have single antenna models.
- you don't touch anybody's musical instrument including your own.
- your pets that move out of the house and start attending college.
- you enjoy the squeak of rusty door hinges.

I'm thinking about selling my Theremin.

I haven't touched it in years.

111

Triangle

I play triangle for a reggae band. It's pretty casual.

I just stand at the back and ting.

They say that the instrument you choose reflects who you are…

I chose triangle.

I was going to take up the triangle,

but I couldn't see the point.

I was asked to try out for triangle in the local orchestra.

I thought I might as well give it a bash.

Trombone

It is difficult to trust anyone whose instrument changes shape as he plays it!

How do you get a trombonist off your doorstep?

Pay for the pizza.

How do you reduce wind-drag on a trombonist's car?

Take the Domino's sign off the roof.

What do you call a beautiful woman on a trombonist's arm?

A tattoo.

Trombone: a slide whistle with delusions of grandeur.

Two trombonists walked out of a bar…

What's the difference between a dead chicken in the road, and a dead trombonist in the road?

There's a remote chance the chicken was on its way to a gig.

What's the latest crime wave in New York City?

Drive-by trombone solos.

What is another term for trombone?

A wind driven, manually operated, pitch approximator.

What is the dynamic range of a bass trombone?

On or off.

Why do people play trombone?

Because they can't move their fingers and read music at the same time.

What's the definition of optimism?

A bass trombonist with a beeper.

Conductor: "When you play that phrase it should sound like the heavens opening, like all of humanity crying out with joy."

Trombonist: "So do you want it louder or softer?"

What's the difference between a trombone and a chainsaw?

It's still easier to improvise on a chainsaw.

What is the definition of a gentleman?

A man who knows how to play the trombone, but doesn't.

How do you know when a trombone player is at your door?

The doorbell drags.

How can you tell which kid on a playground is the child of a trombonist?

He doesn't know how to use the slide, and he can't swing.

What do you call a documentary about trombone players?

A slide show.

What is the trombonist's definition of a super tonic?

A tonic that comes with the gin already in it.

What happened to the trombonist's estate after he died?

The second chair trombonist got his jacket and all twelve dollars went to the drummer.

How does a trombone teacher charge for lessons?

On a sliding scale.

Trumpet

How does one trumpet player greet another?

"Hi. I'm better than you."

How many trumpet players does it take to pave a driveway?

Seven, if you lay them out correctly.

What's the difference between a jet aircraft and a trumpet?

About three decibels.

What's the difference between a Trumpet player and the rear end of a horse?

I don't know either.

How are trumpet players like pirates?

They're both murder on the high Cs.

What's the difference between trumpet players and government bonds?

Government bonds eventually mature and earn money.

What do you do with a tone-deaf trumpeter?

Take away his trumpet, give him a pair of sticks, and make him a drummer.

Why can't a gorilla play trumpet?

He's too sensitive.

Why do trumpeters always sit at the front of the plane?

In the event of a nose dive, the drinks trolley is sure to come past one last time!

Tuba

Tuba Player: "Did you hear my last recital?"

Friend: "I hope so."

How do you fix a broken brass instrument?

With a tuba glue.

What do you call a tuba Player correctly noticing the key signature?

Astute.

What's the range of a tuba?

About twenty yards if you've got a good arm and there's a tail wind!

How many tuba players does it take to change a light bulb?

Three! One to hold the bulb and two to drink 'till the room spins.

How many tuba players does it take to change a light bulb?

Ten. One to change it, and nine to congratulate him down at the pub afterwards.

There are two tuba players sitting in the car. Who's driving?

The policeman.

Turntables

Two DJ's are talking about the evening, the first says "wanna go see a movie tonight?"

The other replies "dunno, who's the projectionist?"

A DJ was asked for a request.

He replied: "Is that to eat in or to go?"

Ukulele

How many ukulele players does it take to cover an Iz song?

All of them, apparently.

Why aren't banjo ukuleles popular?

They take twice as long to burn.

What did the guitar say to the ukulele?

Uke, I am your father.

How do you stop a bus load of ukulele players from going over a cliff?

You don't!

Viola

What's the difference between a viola and an onion?

No one cries when you cut up a viola.

What do a viola and a lawsuit have in common?

Everyone is relieved when the case is closed.

How can you tell if a viola is playing out of tune?

The bow moves.

How does a violist's brain cell die?

Alone.

How do you stop your violin being stolen?

Put it in a viola case.

Why are violist's fingers like lightning?

They rarely strike the same spot twice.

Why don't violists play hide and seek?

Because nobody would look for them.

Glissando: A technique adopted by violists for difficult runs.

What's the definition of perfect pitch?

When you throw a viola into the toilet and it doesn't hit the sides.

What's the difference between a dog and a violist?

A dog knows when to stop scratching.

What's the difference between a Lawnmower and a Viola?

Vibrato.

A violin and a viola are both in a burning building, in the same room, which burns first?

The violin because the viola was still in its case.

A violist was in the back seat of a small town's orchestra.

One day he found a genie and was granted three wishes.

The first wish was that he wanted to be 5 times better then he already was. By the next practice he was principal of the violists.

After some time, he wanted to become even better. He went to the genie and asked to be 10 times better once more. The next day he became the principal violist of the Chicago Symphony Orchestra.

After months he still wanted to become a musician. He asked the genie once more but to be 15 times better. The next day at practice he was back in his small town's orchestra, but in the very back of the second violin section.

What's the difference between the violin section and the viola section of an orchestra?

About half a bar.

A viola player goes to a convenience store to get a drink.

However, just as he is paying, he realizes that he left his case out in plain view.

He rushed back to his car, but it was already too late... someone had already broken in and left 3 more violas.

A viola player went to a piano recital.

After the performance he went up to the pianist and said, "You know, I particularly liked that piece you played last, the one that started with a long trill."

The pianist said, "Huh? I didn't play any pieces that started with trills."

The viola player said, "You know–[he hums the opening bars of Für Elise.]"

The difference between violin and viola is that the viola is a violin with a college education.

Why is a violist like a SCUD missile?

Both are offensive and inaccurate.

What's the difference between a seamstress and a violist?

The seamstress tucks up the frills.

What is the definition of a major seventh?

A violist playing octaves.

How do you make a violist play vibrato?

Write a whole note and put "SOLO" over it.

How do you make a violin sound like a viola?

Sit in the back and don't play.

What instrument do violists envy most?

The harp. You only ever have to play pizzicato on open strings.

Why is a violist like a terrorist?

They both screw up bowings.

What do you do with a dead violist?

Move him back a desk.

What's another name for viola auditions?

Scratch lottery.

What do the Beatles and the LSO viola section have in common?

Neither has played together since 1970.

How was the canon invented?

Two violists were trying to play the same passage together.

Who makes the best viola mutes?

Smith & Wesson.

How does a composer create an orchestral glissando effect?

Write a 16th note run for the violas.

What is the difference between a radio and a viola?

A radio plays music.

What's the only thing a violinist can do better than a violist?

Play the viola.

How many Violists does it take to prepare a batch of chocolate chip cookies?

Three. One to stir the dough, two to peel the M&Ms.

A violist came home and found his house burned to the ground.

When he asked what happened, the police told him "Well, apparently the conductor came to your house, and …"

The violist's eyes lit up and he interrupted excitedly, "The conductor? Came to my house?"

FOR SALE Viola: German, 19th century, 405mm. Excellent condition. Recently tuned.

A violist and a percussionist were walking in a park.

The percussionist saw a dead crow and said to the violist, "Look, a dead crow."

The violist looked up and asked, "Where?"

The string quartet always rehearsed at the home of the first violinist.

The violist kept on inviting the others to rehearse at his place once in a while, and finally, the others agreed to do so.

When they arrived at the violist's house, they found a large and completed jigsaw puzzle sitting on the table in the study.

They admired it and one of the members of the quartet asked their host how long it had taken to put it together. The violist replied, "Six months."

"Six months?" asked the cellist. "Why so long?"

The violist looked shocked. "I thought that was quite an accomplishment! The box said '2 to 3 years'!"

What do you call a person who plays the viola?

A violator.

Violin

How many 2nd violinists does it take to change a light bulb?

None, they can't get up that high !!!!!!

Why do violinists put a cloth between their chin and their instrument?

Violins don't have spit valves.

Why are violas larger than violins?

They aren't. The violin just looks smaller because the violinist's head is so much bigger.

Why are viola jokes so short?

So violinists can understand them.

What's the difference between a violin and a fiddle?

A fiddle is fun to listen to.

Why should you never try to drive a roof nail with a violin?

You might bend the nail.

A first violinist, a second violinist, a virtuoso violist, and a bass player are at the four corners of a football field.

At the signal, someone drops a 100 dollar bill in the middle of the field and they run to grab it. Who gets it?

The second violinist, because:

1. No first violinist is going anywhere for only 100 dollars.
2. There's no such thing as a virtuoso violist.
3. The bass player hasn't figured out what it's all about.

Three violin manufactures have all done business for years on the same block in the small town of Cremona, Italy.

After years of a peaceful co-existence, the Amati shop decided to put a sign in the window saying: "We make the best violins in Italy."

The Guarneri shop soon followed suit, and put a sign in their window proclaiming: "We make the best violins in the world."

Finally, the Stradivarius family put a sign out at their shop saying: "We make the best violins on the block."

Whistle

How can you tell the difference between whistle tunes?

By the names.

Definition of accidental:

Two tin whisle players playing in harmony.

What's the first tune a tin whistler is asked to play?

Over the hills and far away.

If a tin whistle is made of tin, what is a foghorn made of?

Xylophone

I asked my local campanologist if he knew what a xylophone was?

He said it didn't ring a bell.

What type of phone can't be used to call a friend?

A xylophone!

What's the difference between a glockenspiel and a xylophone?

I can't marimba.

Yehu

Does a yehu player play a Han solo?

Zither

How many zither players does it take to screw in a light bulb?

Anywhere from 19 to 72.

What do you call a zither mounted on the hood of your car?

An autoharp.

Which is more frustrating, a zither or chess?

A zither; it's easy to find someone to show you how to play chess.

Why did the idiot decide to take up zither?

To get rich.

What do you call a zither at the bottom of the ocean?

A good start.

What do you call a zither on dry land?

Kindling.

The zither duo gave up on their ambition of becoming a trio.

They couldn't find the third man.

When does a zither sound its most beautiful?

When it's softly crackling in the fireplace.

The most requested piece in the zither repertoire:

John Cage's 4'33"

Weapons of Mass Destruction

Advice from the Pentagon's list of band weapons:

PICCOLO:

The minute dimensions of this weapon make it especially lethal, as it is easily concealed and can be set off just about anywhere. As a solo weapon, this device emits a high-pitched squeal that directly targets the inner ear. The application of this tone temporarily disorients its intended victim rendering him unable to react.

The natural reaction of covering one's ears to reduce the intense pain causes military personnel within a 100 yard radius to drop their weapons leaving them defenceless to further attack. Applied in concert with a second piccolo of slightly higher or lower pitch, the weapons produce the effect of an ice pick through the eardrum and may cause profuse bleeding of the aural cavity.

These weapons are constructed in three forms; metal, composite materials, wood, or any combination of the three. The all-metal piccolos are especially lethal.

The only countermeasure to this weapon is to apply psychological warfare in the following manner. Compliment the musician on her: clothes/hair/shoes. This will distract the musician(s) from emitting her deadly tones and cause her to gab endlessly about herself. This in itself takes us to another problem man has dealt with for a thousand years and to which there is no antidote. Good Luck!

FLUTE:

Slightly less effective than the piccolo but still nothing to be trifled with. The flute possesses the same destructive qualities as the piccolo but is required in greater numbers to do so.

Sixth and seventh grade females are especially effective with this weapon and are to be approached with extreme caution.

OBOE:

This weapon appears harmless at first sight. The instrument's stealth qualities lure victims into a false state of security, and then hit them without mercy. The oboe itself is a harmless composite or wooden conical tube. Once the reed is inserted, it is a weapon of tremendous power.

One comforting factor is that the oboe is only as dangerous as the musician who wields it. At first glance, the operator of the oboe appears sweet, demure, and approachable. Do not be fooled by this deception. The oboist is actually a very high strung and temperamental foe, caused by the perpetual search for the perfect reed, which we all know doesn't exist.

Those who play on plastic reeds are the bottom dwellers of the oboe world and are especially dangerous. The oboe is capable of producing a tone of laser-like quality. The sheer capabilities of volume produced can overpower an entire concert band.

The resulting back pressure produced by over blowing has a two-way effect. It allows the musician to play seemingly forever on one breath resulting in sympathetic vibrations causing bulletproof glass and diamonds to shatter into deadly flying shards.

The warning signs of impending doom occur when the musician raises the body of the instrument to her mouth to blow dust from under a key. This is how the weapon is cocked. If you ever see an oboist do this, run for cover my friend, for all Hell is about to break loose.

The second effect of this weapon's back pressure is to cause its owner to eventually go insane. On rare occasions an oboist's head has been known to explode while firing their weapon.

The only countermeasure to this weapon is to remove and professionally destroy the reed. This will incur the wrath of its owner, so use extreme caution. The first master of the oboe as a weapon was Melvin "Schwartz" (Oklahoma All-State Band 1982). He single handedly destroyed a performance of the Howard Hanson Romantic Symphony Finale under McBeth with his laser-like tones and inconsistent attacks. He still has a bounty on his head and was last seen tending bar in Tijuana.

Eb CLARINET:

The Eb clarinet is the Tasmanian Devil of the woodwind family. Entirely uncontrollable and unpredictable, its blunderbuss like emissions can occur without warning. It is as much a danger to its owner as it is to the intended victim. For this reason the Eb clarinet is not in wide use today and only used by highly trained professionals and circus band daredevils.

Bb CLARINET:

As the flute is to the piccolo, the Bb Clarinet is to the Eb Clarinet. A Bb clarinet is only considered truly dangerous in the hands of a saxophonist doubling on clarinet. His seeming inability to adjust air to the clarinet causes a tone so horrific that decorum prevents me from continuing.

ALTO, BASS, CONTRA BASS CLARINET:

Scud missiles of the clarinet family. Considered low-grade weapons, these are of limited lethality due to the extreme geekiness of their operators.

BASSOON:

A weapon designed to start wars. Used primarily indoors, this weapon's unique tone can cause great embarrassment in social situations.

Known as the "farting bed post" the bassoonist will hide behind a set of curtains at an official state dinner or similar function. With the help of a diplomatic operative during the meal, the flatulent tones emitted by the bassoon can be blamed on visiting high government officials, causing great embarrassment and the possible beginning of hostilities..

The best bassoon countermeasure involves lighter fluid and matches.

SOPRANO SAXOPHONE:

(See Kenny G) AHHHHHHHHHRGHHH!!!!!

ALTO SAX:

Originally invented by Adolphe Sax as the result of an evening of much cheap wine and a dare by a drunken horn player, the instrument he produced is neither brass nor woodwind.

The only intended victim of this vile weapon is the concert band French horn player. Nothing is worse than hearing a great brass lick only to be obscured by the overly reedy tone and wobbly "vibrato" of some half crazed alto sax doubling the horns and overplaying them.

Composers and arrangers are to blame as much as alto players. Older players unable to temper their '40's swing band vibrato are also a danger.

The only counter measure is to question their manhood by daring the player to play Charlie Parker's "Donna Lee" at 230 beats per minute. That should shut 'em up!

TENOR SAX:

(See Alto Sax) Counter measure, throw down the gauntlet with a dare to render John Coltrane's "Giant Steps".

BARITONE SAX:

A tenor or alto wannabe, this instrument is flaccid and harmless unless played in the style of Stephen "Doc" Kupka (Tower of Power). His sporadic well placed grunting and punctuated style, when discovered by young players, can cause discomfort among the average school director.

The only counter measure to this is self-medication by the teacher in the form of tequila shots or similar substances.

TRUMPET:

Obviously one would think that a trumpeter's greatest weapon is his ability to play high notes at great volume. This misconception has been perpetuated unwittingly by great performers like Maynard Ferguson and Dizzy Gillespie. The danger is not in the player who can play high. The danger lies in the player who THINKS he can play high. A young player's incessant caterwauling and inflated ego are a danger to himself and all those around him.

The most effective counter measure is to allow the player to continue his high note practice (even encourage him to go higher and louder) until his lips explode or he cracks a tooth jamming his face into the mouthpiece.

FRENCH HORN:

French horns thankfully are a danger only to a small group of people, as their bells point in the wrong direction. They are only a danger to those unfortunate enough to have to sit behind them.

Their intonation problems and constant cracking of pitches is of great annoyance to those brass players sitting behind them. Though lately the introduction of Plexiglas reflectors has reduced the danger to those behind the horns, unfortunately it presents a greater danger to the players themselves and those in front of them.

Upon hearing their actual tones coming back at them, some hornists have been known to vomit on stage due to the hideousness of their own tone.

TROMBONE:

A unique application, the instrument itself is not the real danger. The person playing the instrument is what is truly dangerous. The trombone and its player are the original "smart bomb."

This weapon is most effective in high tech warfare areas. Insertion of one or more trombonists into a computer center instantly lowers the aggregate I.Q. in the room. The trombonist's incredible stupidity is a lethal bio weapon that spreads at an incredible rate. Within 5 minutes of exposure, all computer operators within a 50-foot radius are reduced to drooling idiots incapable of the simplest motor functions and bowel control.

Use of trombonists as weapons was outlawed by the Geneva Convention in 1999 after an ugly incident at a Dixieland convention in Sacramento.

BARITONE/EUPHONIUM:

This is a weapon of mass confusion. Euphonium players are the Rodney Dangerfields of the brass world. Young players especially don't know their place in the band. They double French horns, trombones, saxophones, tubas in octaves, bass clarinets, bassoons…yadda, yadda, yadda! Euphonium orchestral parts are played by the second trombone or worse, the tuba player!

For this reason most euphonium.........baritone… (WHATEVER!) players resort to doubling on trombone. This is when they become dangerous. (See trombone.)

TUBA:

This is a sonic weapon that when set off can produce sub sonic tones causing a general feeling of uneasiness and queasiness to those within its effective range. In addition, one may attach a sousaphone to a marching column of soldiers.

As all tubists drag, the ever-slowing performance of um-pahs will eventually reduce the marching soldiers to a snail's pace causing them to be late for a battle or not arrive at all.

The most effective countermeasure is to feed the tubist with great quantities of beer (imports if you have them). It won't improve his playing but makes him more enjoyable to be around.

SNARE DRUM/TRAP SET:

This weapon affects only a very small demographic: teenage girls and the fathers of these girls with steady jobs and liquid bank accounts. The snare drummer and the jazz/rock variety of set player act almost like a computer worm. The drummer will attach himself to an unsuspecting teenage girl and milk her and her father's finances in such a way as to not be noticed by the father until it is too late.

Drummers are the leeches of the music world and can only be countered by being forced to get a real day job. This will reduce the drummer's "coolness" factor and the daughter will immediately lose interest.

Musical Limericks

A pianist named Jimmy O'Dougherty
played jazz on an old piano-forte.
He played on and on,
made the audience yawn,
and died on stage when he was forty.

There once was a zebra from China.
Who liked to sing songs in D minor.
His voice was the rage
When they put him on stage.
He rode out of town a headliner!

There was a composer named Mozart
Whose music's okay (for the most part)
From the scraping of strings
To the thumping on things
To the large-people-stretching-their-throats part.

There was a composer, Nancarrow
Whose musical breadth was quite narrow.
But all is explained,
See, at birth he'd obtained
A brain that was meant for a sparrow.

A man who had played the bassoon
was heard whistling a hillbilly tune.
And although it's not fair
He was moved from first chair,
and forbidden to play Claire de Lune.

A bass player named Waldo Hippen
said, "Frankly, for long-distance shippin',
I'd prefer a French horn:
It's more easily borne,
And it's nice to put crackers and dip in."

I've never heard songs any finer
Than Schubert's late settings of Heine.
Die Stadt, with its edgy
Piano arpeggi,
Sounds best in the key of C minor.

A guitarist named Pat Donohue
Said, "Guitar is ideal, in my view.
I find it attracts
lots more girls than a sax,
And the neighbours are fond of it, too."

There once was a cycle, The Ring
With music, and plenty to sing.
There's not a note wrong,
But it was so long
That nobody's heard the whole thing.

There was an old crooner named Geoff
Who got gradually more and more deaf
Til he couldn't distinguish
Italian from English
Or the treble, alto or bass clef.

A symphony cellist named Kate
Shares her stand with a man, once her date.
Though they play well in sync,
She now thinks him a fink
And longs for his move out of state.

But orchestra jobs are quite rare,
And he can't find a gig anywhere.
Sadly, neither can she,
So together they'll be
Making music. At least she's first chair.

"Your playing is way out of tune,"
A conductor informed the bassoon.
"All your high notes are sharp,
And I don't mean to carp,
But you sound like a horny baboon".

The bassoonist replied, "Sir, your ear
Gets progressively worse ev'ry year,
And your cues are all wrong,
So we just play along
And pretend your baton waving's clear."

"Your CD collection's a joke,
And classical sucks," yelled the bloke.
My discs couldn't handle
This rampaging vandal:
Now all of my Bach sets are broke.

There was a composer named Cage
whose music was once all the rage.
It was nothing but bunk
and it certainly stunk,
but people still thought him a sage!

A conductor, thought he was elite,
But in substance, was always off beat.
He pressured musicians
With harsh admonitions,
but to follow his stick was a feat.

A soprano who crooned out of key
Did it loudly with pleasure and glee.
She believed she sang well,
Like a beautiful bell.
But "please stop," was the usual plea.

Musical Definitions

- **Accent:** An unusual manner of pronunciation, e.g.: "Y'all sang that real good!"
- **Accidentals:** Wrong notes.
- **Ad Libitum:** A premiere.
- **Agitato:** A string player's state of mind when a peg slips in the middle of a piece, or when a brass player's valve sticks.
- **Agnus Dei:** A woman composer famous for her church music.
- **Allegro:** Leg fertilizer.
- **Altered Chord:** A sonority that has been spayed.
- **Altos:** not to be confused with "Tom's toes," "Bubba's toes" or "Dori-toes".
- **Arpeggio:** "Ain't he that storybook kid with the big nose that grows?"
- **Atonality:** Disease that many modern composers suffer from. The most prominent symptom is the patient's lacking ability to make decisions.
- **Attaca:** "Fire at will!"
- **Audition:** the act of putting oneself under extreme duress to satisfy the sadistic intentions of someone who has already made up his mind.
- **Augmented Fifth:** A 36-ounce bottle.
- **Bach Chorale:** the place behind the barn where you keep the horses.
- **Bar Line:** A gathering of people, usually among which may be found a musician or two.
- **Bass Clef:** where you wind up if you do fall off.
- **Bass:** the things you run around in softball.

- **Beat:** What music students to do each other with their musical instruments. The down beat is performed on the top of the head, while the up beat is struck under the chin.
- **Big Band:** when the bar pays enough to bring two banjo players.
- **Bravo:** Literally, How bold! or What nerve! This is a spontaneous expression of appreciation on the part of the concert goer after a particularly trying performance.
- **Breve:** The way a sustained note sounds when a violinist runs out of bow.
- **Broken Consort:** When somebody in the ensemble has to leave and go to the restroom.
- **Cadence:**
  1. The short nickname of a rock group whose full name is Cadence Clearwater Revival.
  2. When everybody hopes you're going to stop, but you don't. (Final Cadence when they FORCE you to stop.)
- **Cadenza:** The heroine in Monteverdi's opera "Frottola".
- **Cantus Firmus:** The part you get when you can only play four notes.
- **Cello:** the proper way to answer the phone.
- **Chansons De Geste:** Dirty songs.
- **Chord:** Usually spelled with an "s" on the end, means a particular type of pants, e.g. "He wears chords."
- **Chromatic Scale:** An instrument for weighing that indicates half-pounds.
- **Clarinet:** name used on your second daughter if you've already used Betty Jo.
- **Clausula:** Mrs. Santa.

153

- **Clef:**
  1. If a student cannot sing, he may have an affliction of the palate, called a clef.
  2. Something to jump from if you can't sing and you have to teach elementary school.
- **Coloratura Soprano:** A singer who has great trouble finding the proper note, but who has a wild time hunting for it.
- **Compound Meter:** A place to park your car that requires two dimes.
- **Con Brio:** Done with scouring pads and washboards.
- **Conduct:** The type of air vents in a prison, especially designed to prevent escape. Could also be installed for effective use in a practice room.
- **Conductor:** A musician who is adept at following many people at the same time.
- **Counterpoint:** A favorite device of many Baroque composers, all of whom are dead, though no direct connection between these two facts has been established. Still taught in many schools, as a form of punishment.
- **Countertenor:** A singing waiter.
- **Crescendo:** A reminder to the performer that he has been playing too loudly.
- **Crotchet:** A tritone with a bent prong - or, It's like knitting but it's faster.
- **Cut Time:** When you're going twice as fast as everyone else in the orchestra.
- **Cymbal:** what they use on deer-crossing signs so you know what to sight-in your pistol with.

- **Da capo al fine:** I like your hat!
- **Detache:** An indication that the trombones are to play with the slides removed.
- **Di Lasso:** Popular with Italian cowboys.

154

- **Diatonic:** Low-calorie Schweppes.
- **Diminished fifth:** An empty bottle of Jack Daniels.
- **Discord:** Not to be confused with Datcord.
- **Dominant:** An adjective used to describe the voice of a child who sings off key.
- **Ductia:** A lot of mallards.
- **Duple Meter:** May take any even number of coins.
- **Duration:** Can be used to describe how long a music teacher can exercise self-control.
- **Embouchre:** The way you look when you've been playing the Krummhorn.
- **English Horn:** Neither English nor a horn, not to be confused with the French Horn, which is German.
- **Espressivo:** Close eyes and play with a wide vibrato.
- **Estampie:** What they put on letters in Quebec.
- **Fermata:** A brand of girdle made especially for opera singers.
- **Fermented fifth:** What the percussion players keep behind the tympani, which resolves to a 'distilled fifth', which is what the conductor uses backstage.
- **Fine:** That was great!
- **First Inversion:** grandpa's battle group at Normandy.
- **Flat:** This is what happens to a tonic if it sits too long in the open air.
- **Flute:** A sophisticated pea shooter with a range of up to 500 yards, blown transversely to confuse the enemy.
- **Form:**
  1. The shape of a composition.
  2. The shape of the musician playing the composition.
  3. The people of paper to be filled out in triplicate in order to get enough money from the Arts Council to play the composition.
- **French horn:** Your wife says you smell like a cheap one when you come in at 4 a.m.

155

- **Garglefinklein:** A tiny recorder played by neums
- **Glissando:**
  1. The musical equivalent of slipping on a banana peel.
  2. A technique adopted by string players for difficult runs.
- **Gregorian chant:** A way of singing in unison, invented by monks to hide snoring.
- **Half Step:** The pace used by a cellist when carrying his instrument.
- **Harmonic Minor:** A good music student.
- **Harmony:** A corn-like food eaten by people with accents (see above for definition of accent).
- **Hemiola:** A hereditary blood disease caused by chromatics.
- **Heroic Tenor:** A singer who gets by on sheer nerve and tight clothing.
- **Hocket:** The thing that fits into a crochet to produce a rackett.
- **Hurdy-gurdy:** A truss for medieval percussionists who get Organistrum.
- **Interval:** How long it takes you to find the right note. There are three kinds: Major Interval - A long time; Minor Interval - A few bars; Inverted Interval - When you have to back one bar and try again.
- **Intonation:** Singing through one's nose. Considered highly desirable in the Middle Ages.
- **Isorhythmic Motet:** When half of the ensemble got a different xerox than the other half.
- **Lamentoso:** With handkerchiefs.
- **Lasso:** The 6th and 5th steps of a descending scale.
- **Lauda:** The difference between shawms and krummhorns.
- **Major Triad:** The name of the head of the Music Department.

- **Mean-Tone Temperament:** One's state of mind when everybody's trying to tune at the same time.
- **Messiah:** An oratorio by Handel performed every Christmas by choirs that believe they are good enough, in co-operation with musicians who need the money.
- **Meter Signature:** The name of the maid who writes you a ticket when you put an odd number of coins in a duple meter.
- **Metronome:** A smurf in the Paris underground.
- **Minnesinger:** A boy soprano.
- **Minor Triad:** The name of the wife of the head of the Music Department.
- **Modulation:** "Nothing is bad in modulation."
- **Music:** A complex organizations of sounds that is set down by the composer, incorrectly interpreted by the conductor, who is ignored by the musicians, the result of which is ignored by the audience.
- **Musica Ficta:** When you lose your place and have to bluff till you find it again. Also known as faking.

- **Neumatic Melisma:** A bronchial disorder caused by hockets.
- **Neums:** Renaissance smurfs.
- **Oboe:** An ill wind that nobody blows good.
- **Opera:** When a guy gets stabbed in the back and instead of bleeding, he sings.
- **Opus:** A penguin in Kansas.
- **Orchestral Suites:** Naughty women who follow touring orchestras.
- **Ordo:** The hero in Tolkien's "Lord of the Rings" (Snaps for Frodo).
- **Organistrum:** A job-related hazard for careless medieval percussionists, caused by getting one's tapper caught in the clapper.

- **Passing Tone:** frequently heard near the baked beans at family barbecues.
- **Pause:** A short period in an individual voice in which there should be relative quiet. Useful when turning to the next page in the score, breathing, emptying the horn of salvia, coughing, etc. Is rarely heard in baroque music. Today, the minimum requirements for pauses in individual pieces are those of the Musicians' Union (usually one per bar, or 15 minutes per hour).
- **Perfect fifth:** A full bottle of Jack Daniels.
- **Perfect Pitch:** the smooth coating on a freshly paved road.
- **Performance Practise:** Sex education.
- **Pianissimo:** "refill this beer bottle".
- **Plague:** a collective noun, as in "a plague of conductors."
- **Pneumatic melisma:** A bronchial disorder caused by hockets.
- **Portamento:** a foreign country you've always wanted to see.
- **Preparatory beat:** A threat made to singers, i.e. sing, or else....
- **Quaver:** Beginning viol class.

- **Rackett:** Capped reeds class.
- **Recitative:** A disease that Monteverdi had.
- **Relative major:** An uncle in the Marine Corps.
- **Relative minor:** A girlfriend.
- **Repeat:** what you do until they just expel you.
- **Rhythmic drone:** The sound of many monks suffering with Crotchet.
- **Risoluto:** Indicates to orchestras that they are to stubbornly maintain the correct tempo no matter what the conductor tries to do.
- **Ritard:** There's one in every family.
- **Ritornello:** An opera by Verdi.

- **Rota:** An early Italian method of teaching music without score or parts.
- **Rubato:** Expression used to describe irregular behaviour in a performer with sensations of angst in the mating period. Especially common amongst tenors.
- **Sancta:** Clausula's husband.
- **Senza sordino:** A term used to remind the player that he forgot to put his mute on a few measures back.
- **Sine Proprietate:** Cussing in church.
- **Stops:** Something Bach did not have on his organ.
- **String Quartet:** a good violinist, a bad violinist, an ex-violinist, and someone who hates violinists, all getting together to complain about composers.
- **Subito piano:** Indicates an opportunity for some obscure orchestra player to become a soloist.
- **Supertonic:** Schweppes.

- **Tempo:** This is where a headache begins.
- **Tone Cluster:** A chordal orgy first discovered by a well-endowed woman pianist leaning forward for a page turn.
- **Tonic:** Medicinal liquid to be consumed before, during, or after a performance. (Diatonic This is what happens to some musicians.)
- **Transposition:**
  1. An advanced recorder technique where you change from alto to soprano fingering (or vice-versa) in the middle of a piece.
  2. The act of moving the relative pitch of a piece of music that is too low for the basses to a point where it is too high for the sopranos.
- **Transsectional:** an alto who moves to the soprano section.
- **Treble:** women ain't nothin' but.
- **Trill:** The musical equivalent of an epileptic seizure.
- **Triple Meter:** Only rich people should park by these.

- **Triplet:** One of three children, born to one mother very closely in time. If a composer uses a lot of triplets he has probably been taking a fertility drug.
- **Trope:** a malevolent neum.
- **Trotto:** An early Italian form of Montezuma's Revenge.
- **Tuba:** a compound word - "Hey, woman! Fetch me another tuba Bryll Cream!"
- **Tutti:** A lot of sackbuts.
- **Vibrato:**
  1. The singer's equivalent of an epileptic seizure.
  2. Used by singers to hide the fact that they are on the wrong pitch.
- **Virtuoso:** A musician with very high morals.

Subliminal Messages from Composers

Antonín Leopold Dvořák

No! Do not learn viola!

Heitor Villa-Lobos

He boos viola trill

Nicolai Rimsky-Korsakov

OK man, rock viola is risky!

Peter Illyich Tchaikovsky

Check viola key: triply sh**!

Ludwig Van Beethoven

Dun't neveh' be viola!

How to Sing the Blues

Most Blues begin, "Woke up this morning."

"I got a good woman" is a bad way to begin the Blues, 'less you stick something nasty in the next line, like " I got a good woman, with the meanest face in town."

The Blues is simple. After you get the first line right, repeat it. Then find something that rhymes: "Got a good woman - with the meanest face in town. Got teeth like Margaret Thatcher and she weigh 500 pound."

The Blues are not about choice. You stuck in a ditch, you stuck in a ditch; ain't no way out.

Blues cars: Chevys and Cadillacs and broken-down trucks. Blues don't travel in Volvos, BMWs, or Sport Utility Vehicles. Most Blues transportation is a Greyhound bus or a southbound train. Jet aircraft an' state-sponsored motor pools ain't even in the running. Walkin' plays a major part in the blues lifestyle. So does fixin' to die.

Teenagers can't sing the Blues. They ain't fixin' to die yet. Adults sing the Blues. In Blues, " adulthood" means being old enough to get the electric chair if you shoot a man in Memphis.

Blues can take place in New York City but not in Hawaii or any place in Canada. Hard times in St. Paul or Tucson is just depression. Chicago, St. Louis, and Kansas City still the best places to have the Blues. You cannot have the blues in any place that don't get rain.

A man with male pattern baldness ain't the blues. A woman with male pattern baldness is. Breaking your leg cuz you skiing is not the blues. Breaking your leg cuz an alligator be chomping on it is.

You can't have no Blues in an office or a shopping mall. The lighting is wrong. Go outside to the parking lot or sit by the dumpster.

Good places for the Blues:
• highway
• jailhouse
• empty bed

Bad places for the Blues:
• Ashrams
• gallery openings
• Ivy League institutions
• golf courses

No one will believe it's the Blues if you wear a suit, 'less you happen to be an old man, and you slept in it.

You do have the right to sing the Blues if:

* you're older than dirt
* you're blind
* you shot a man in Memphis
* you can't be satisfied

You do **not** have the right to sing the Blues if:

* you have all your teeth
* you were once blind but now can see
* the man in Memphis lived.
* you have a retirement plan or trust fund.

Blues is not a matter of color. It's a matter of bad luck. Tiger Woods cannot sing the blues. Gary Coleman could.

If you ask for water and Baby give you gasoline, it's the Blues.

Other acceptable Blues beverages are:

* muddy water
* black coffee
* bourbon

The following are **NOT** Blues beverages:

* Snapple
* sparkling water
* prosecco

164

If it occurs in a cheap motel or a shotgun shack, it's a Blues death. Stabbed in the back by a jealous lover is another Blues way to die. So is the electric chair, and dying lonely on a broken down cot. You can't have a Blues death if you die during a tennis match or getting liposuction.

Some Blues names for women:

- Sadie
- Big Mama
- Bessie
- Fat River Dumpling

Some Blues names for men:

- Joe
- Willie
- Little Willie
- Big Willie

Persons with names like Sierra, Sequoia, Auburn, and Rainbow can't sing the Blues no matter how many men they shoot in Memphis.

Make your own Blues name (starter kit):

- name of physical infirmity (Blind, Cripple, Lame, etc.)
- first name (see above) plus name of fruit (Lemon, Lime, Kiwi,etc.)
- last name of President (Jefferson, Johnson, Fillmore, etc.)
  For example, Blind Lime Jefferson, or Cripple Kiwi Fillmore, etc. (Well, maybe not "Kiwi.")

I don't care how tragic your life: you own a computer, you cannot sing the blues. You best destroy it. Fire or get out a shotgun. I don't care.

Great Lies of The Music Business

1. The booking is definite
2. Your cheque's in the post
3. We can fix it in the mix
4. This is the best dope you've ever had
5. The show starts at 8
6. My agent will take care of it
7. I'm sure it will work
8. Your tickets are at the door
9. It sounds in tune to me
10. Sure, it sounds fine at the back of the hall
11. I know your mic is on
12. I checked it myself
13. The roadie took care of it
14. She'll be backstage after the show
15. Yes, the spotlight was on you during your solo
16. The stage mix sounds just like the program mix
17. It's the hottest pickup I could get
18. The club will provide the PA and lights
19. I really love the band
20. We'll have it ready by tonight
21. We'll have lunch sometime
22. If it breaks, we'll fix it for free
23. We'll let you know
24. I had nothing to do with your marriage breaking up.
25. The place was packed
26. We'll have you back next week
27. Don't worry, you'll be the headliner
28. It's on the truck
29. My last band had a record deal, but we broke up before recording the album
30. Someone will be there early to let you in
31. I've only been playing for a year
32. I've been playing for 20 years
33. We'll have flyers printed tomorrow

34. I'm with the band
35. The band drinks free
36. You'll get your cut tonight
37. We'll supply someone for the door
38. You'll have no problem fitting that bass cabinet in the trunk of your car
39. There'll be lots of roadies when you get there
40. It's totally compatible with your current program
41. You'll have plenty of time for a soundcheck
42. This is one of Jimi's old Strats
43. We'll definitely come to the gig
44. You can depend on me